DIAGRAM

I I

I0142491

THE THIRD IN OUR SERIES OF PRINT
ANTHOLOGIES FEATURING SELECTIONS FROM
YEARS 5 AND 6 OF YOUR PRIMARY PURVEYOR
OF ONLINE TEXT, ART, SOUND & SCHEMATIC
WHICH IS MOSTLY AVAILABLE AT:

HTTP://THEDIAGRAM.COM

DIAGRAM

II

HTTP://THEDIAGRAM.COM

Edited by Ander Monson

— Del Sol Press ◆ Washington, D.C. —

DIAGRAM III: The Third Print Anthology

Ander Monson, Editor. Copyright © 2008 by DIAGRAM. All Rights Reserved.

DEL SOL PRESS, WASHINGTON, D.C.
PAPER ISBN: 978-1-934832-04-2.

First Edition. Cover and Interior Design by Ander Monson.

Much of the material contained herein originally appeared in DIAGRAM, a magazine of text, art, and schematic, which can be found online at <THEDIAGRAM.COM>, mirrored at Web del Sol, <WEBDELSOL.COM>.

Source materials for images are noted in the acknowledgments page towards the end of the book. We have made our best attempts to obtain permission to reprint the images herein; if you are the copyright holder of an image and object to its reproduction in these pages, please contact us.

The cover image is from Carsten Shradin and Gustil Anzenberger's article, "Costs of Infant Carrying in Common Marmosets, Callithrix jacchus: an Experimental Analysis," *Animal Behavior* 62.2, 2001. This book was produced in cooperation with *DIAGRAM* and the New Michigan Press.

HTTP://THEDIAGRAM.COM
HTTP://NEWMICHIGANPRESS.COM

EDITOR@THEDIAGRAM.COM / NMP@THEDIAGRAM.COM

CONTENTS

CONTENTS (CONTINUED)

On this Artifact

THIS IS THE THIRD IN OUR OCCASIONAL PRINT anthology series. It was produced with a significant amount of labor, especially from Dolly Laninga, our Editorial Assistant, who helped greatly with research, selection, compilation, and editing, and who is responsible for finding most of these excellent images.

SELECTIONS FOR THIS ANTHOLOGY were made from the work we've published online from issues 5.1 to 6.6. Our editors individually and collectively chose work specifically that translated well to the printed page, and that we particularly loved. I wish we could have included everything we published online in these twelve issues, but then this book's spine would break under the weight of its glorious pages, thus violating the contract of the book as artifact.

THANKS MUCH TO MY OTHER PARTNERS IN CRIME, particularly Poetry Editor Heidi Gotz, who has been here from the magazine's inception, and our Fiction Editor, Lauren Slaughter. Additional thanks go to Assistant Editors Sarah Blackman, Tom Fleischmann, Emma Ramey, Mike Salisbury, Katie Shinkle, Reviews Editor Aaron Welborn, and Sonics Editor Shannon Fields.

—*Ander Monson, Editor*

(January 2008)

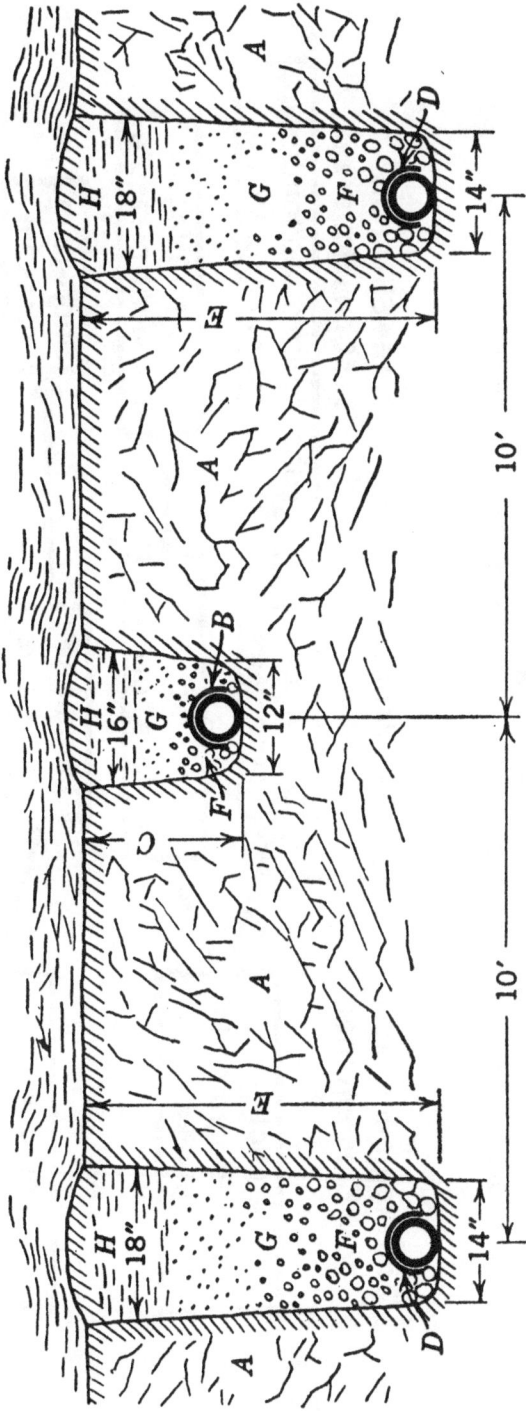

FIG. 81. Close Soils Should be Deeply Subsoiled and Underdrained. (*From U. S. Department of Agriculture, Farmers' Bull. 1227.*)

Diagram 1 • The Mechanism of Unhappiness

Type of Programming: ADDICTIVE (Emotion-backed) PROGRAMMING
Direction of Energy Flow: Manipulating Subject-Object Relationships
Associated Centers of Consciousness: Security, Sensation, and Power Centers

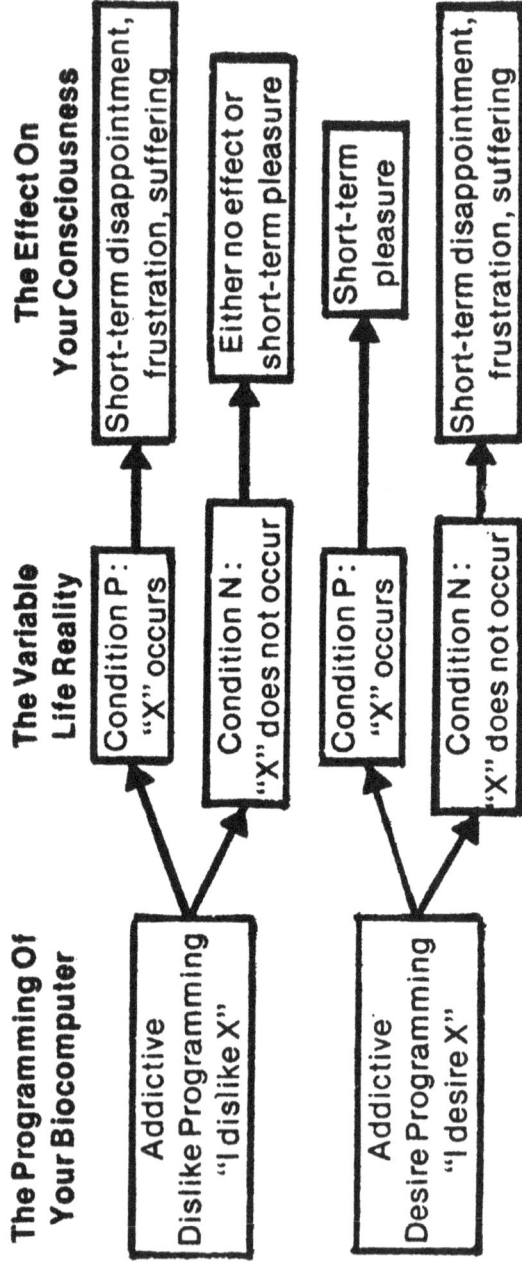

The Programming Of Your Biocomputer	The Variable Life Reality	The Effect On Your Consciousness
Addictive Dislike Programming "I dislike X"	Condition P: "X" occurs	Short-term disappointment, frustration, suffering
	Condition N: "X" does not occur	Either no effect or short-term pleasure
Addictive Desire Programming "I desire X"	Condition P: "X" occurs	Short-term pleasure
	Condition N: "X" does not occur	Short-term disappointment, frustration, suffering

Diagram 2 • The Mechanism of Happiness

Type of Programming: PREFERENTIAL (Non-Emotion-backed) PROGRAMMING
Direction of Energy Flow: Unconditional Acceptance or Love
Associated Centers of Consciousness: Love, Cornucopia, and Conscious-awareness Centers

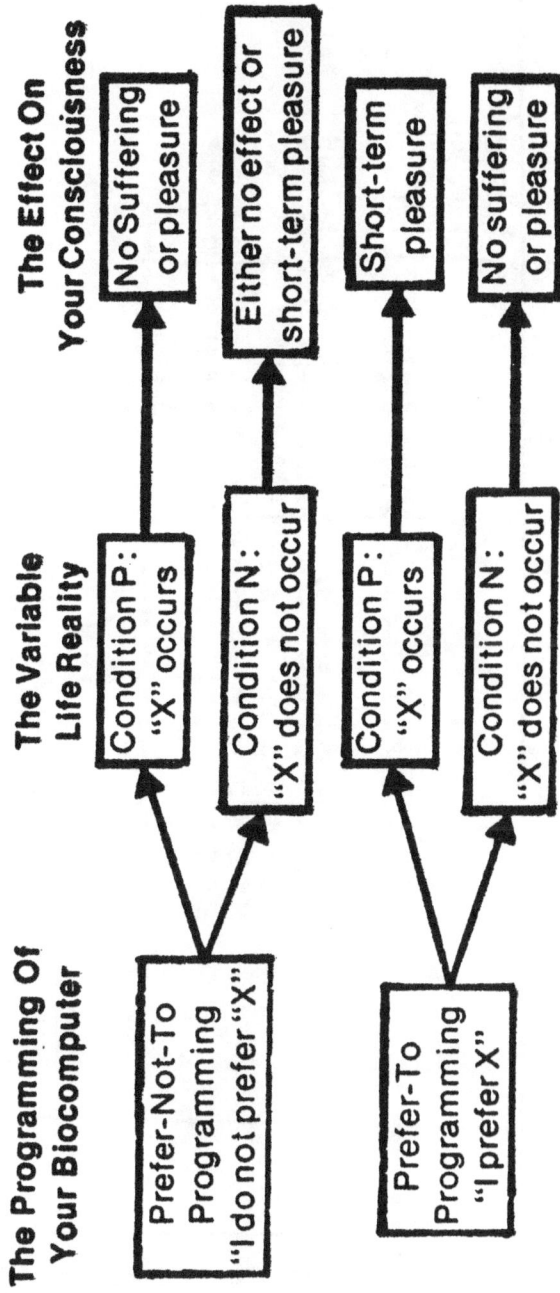

The Programming Of Your Biocomputer	The Variable Life Reality	The Effect On Your Consciousness
Prefer-Not-To Programming "I do not prefer "X""	Condition P: "X" occurs	No Suffering or pleasure
	Condition N: "X" does not occur	Either no effect or short-term pleasure
Prefer-To Programming "I prefer X"	Condition P: "X" occurs	Short-term pleasure
	Condition N: "X" does not occur	No suffering or pleasure

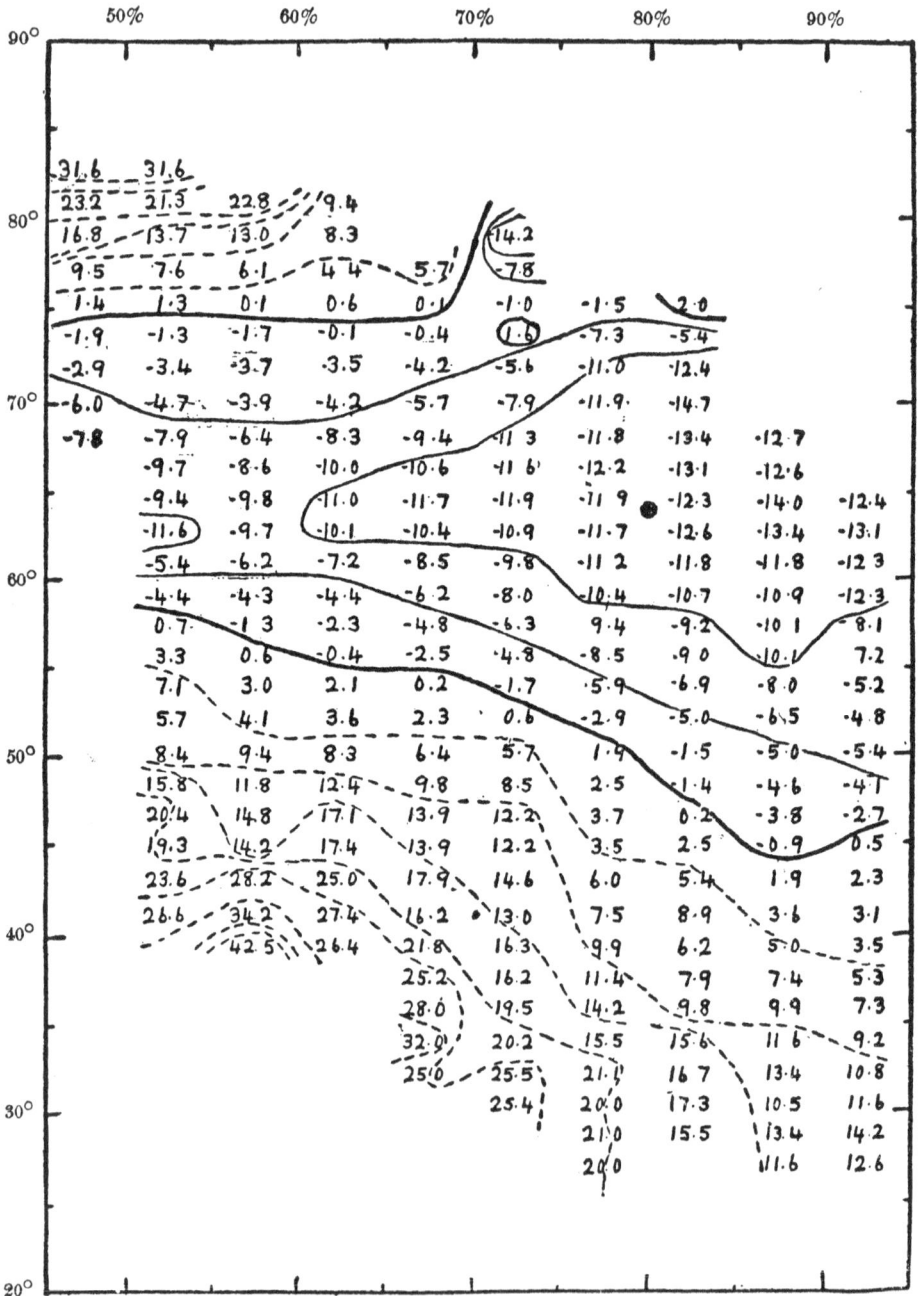

FIGURE 30. Unsmoothed Climograph of France and Italy, 1899-1913, 3,700,000 Deaths

What others are saying about *The Black Dog*

"I just finished reading *The Black Dog* and wanted to say what an extraordinary book this will be.

It was moving, riveting, insightful and honest. I know it will help a multitude of people who are suffering from depression today."

—Venerable Elaine Bellis, Archdeacon of Chicago

"*The Black Dog* is a story using a most appropriate symbol of the struggle that 'hounded' the author from childhood. The illustrations throughout the manuscript capture the insidious nature of the beast as it pursues him throughout his life. Depression and anxiety are familiar agents of mental distress, we learn, which diminish one's capacity for a productive and useful life. They also deeply affect relationships in family, community and the workplace.

The author's telling of his story is deeply engaging and unfolds before this reader curiosity with understandable, vivid descriptions. They are personal and revealing insights into the ongoing battle of a dedicated family man, accomplished professional and ordained Christian minister coming to terms with a debilitating affliction.

In this day and age, no one can escape the problems and pressures of living among the chances and changes that come along daily. For some they are roadblocks, even collisions, with those around us at home, at work, even in Church. But the author's genuine, honest and open telling of his story give hope that with grace, the love of God and others and the willingness to reach out and receive help, a unique, valuable and marvelous person is forged in a man of compassion, supreme value, and a joy to know and love."

—Reverend Thomas P. Rosa, Trinity Episcopal Church, Aurora, IL